A Country AT WAR

The personal experiences of
Private 1228 W. S. Batey
18th Battalion
Northumberland Fusiliers

A COUNTRYMAN AT WAR
1915 – 1919

Dedicated to all the Northumbrians who volunteered to serve their King and Country in The Great War.

The personal experiences of One Man's War
Private 1228 W. S. Batey
18th Battalion Northumberland Fusiliers.

Acknowledgements

This account was written with the encouragement of my wife Beth, my son Daniel, his wife Gaelle and their children Ewan and Elena. Clive Dalton pressed me to get it completed. Warm thanks are due to Stan Owen for a great deal of help in taking a computer script, putting it into book form and adding illustrations.

© Account prepared by his son, Tom Batey, January 2021

Front cover: Poppies now grow where W. S. Batey once fought.

Apart from any fair dealing for the purposes of research or private study, or criticism or review as permitted under the Copyright, Designs and Patents Act 1988, this publication may not be reproduced, stored or transmitted, in any form or by any means, without the prior permission in writing of the author. Inquiries should be sent to the author c/o The Heritage Centre, Station Yard, Woodburn Road, Bellingham, Northumberland, NE48 2DG.

Foreword

By Dr. Clive Dalton

It is a pleasure to commend Tom's book because, like me, whose father also as a young lad risked death without glory in WW1, one stray bit of German lead or a bayonet could have stopped you reading this great bit of history, or my support for a great story so well told.

The WWI survivors never talked much about the horrors and nightmares they suffered, fighting for a ridiculous cause that Britain need never to have got involved in – the murder of an Austrian Archduke!

Tom's story highlights the character of the young lads of Northumberland, and from all over Britain, which persuaded them to volunteer for a noble cause – and, in any case, that they'd be home safe and sound by Christmas after a great adventure overseas. Hexham would have been as far as most of them ever went, Newcastle on a very rare visit and most would have never seen the sea. The English Channel would have been their first sight and taste of salt water and waves to get them excited – and seasick!

When signing on, they certainly would not have been told much about having to put a bullet in a young German lad their own age or, worse still, sticking a bayonet in him and using your foot on his chest to pull it out as he screamed in agony. The reality of the trenches, the mud, the rats, the lice and the smell of dead men and horses are scary enough to read about in the book – but how folk like Tom's father and thousands more put up with it cannot be imagined.

If you want to fully appreciate what this would have been like, try looking at your children and grandchildren in their late teens and early 20s and think of them being ordered to suffer these horrors! It's a haunting thought, which makes you wonder about the sanity of Homo Sapiens. Sadly, nothing has changed in the DNA of the species.

I won't wish that you get 'enjoyment' from reading about the contribution that Tom's father made in the Great War but I do hope that it will help you think about, and pay tribute to, the Northumbrian lads like Pte 1228 W. S. Batey and others who, for four long years, sacrificed so much of their young lives for our freedom.

Men of the 18th (Service) Battalion Northumberland Fusiliers (1st Tyneside Pioneers)

Please note that the terms Service and Pioneers are synonymous and Pioneers is used throughout this book.

The Military Service of Private 1228 W. S. Batey
18th (Service) Battalion Northumberland Fusiliers

PART 1   pages 6 - 13

Introduction; The Pioneer (Service) Battalions

PART 2   pages 13 - 27

France: 1st Tour of Duty: The Trenches; Deployment; No man's land; Trench Warfare; Injuries; Medical Support; Barbed Wire; The Battle of The Somme; wounded and gassed; hospital, recuperation and return to duty

PART 3   pages 27 - 34

France: 2nd Tour of Duty: buried in a trench; hospital, recuperation and return to duty; Machine Gun Corps; 16th (Service) Battalion; Fatalities; Demobilisation; Post-War Life

PART 4   pages 35 - 40

Summary of War Service; *In Flanders Fields*; Epilogue; The Battle of The Somme Roll of Honour, 18th Battalion Northumberland Fusiliers

PART 5   pages 41 - 47

Renwick Memorial, Newcastle: unveiling (1923) and further details; Parade of "The Commercials" (1915); Bibliography

PART 6   pages 48 - 54

Through a Soldier's Eyes: sights & scenes of the Great War

Well Done, Northumberland Fusiliers!

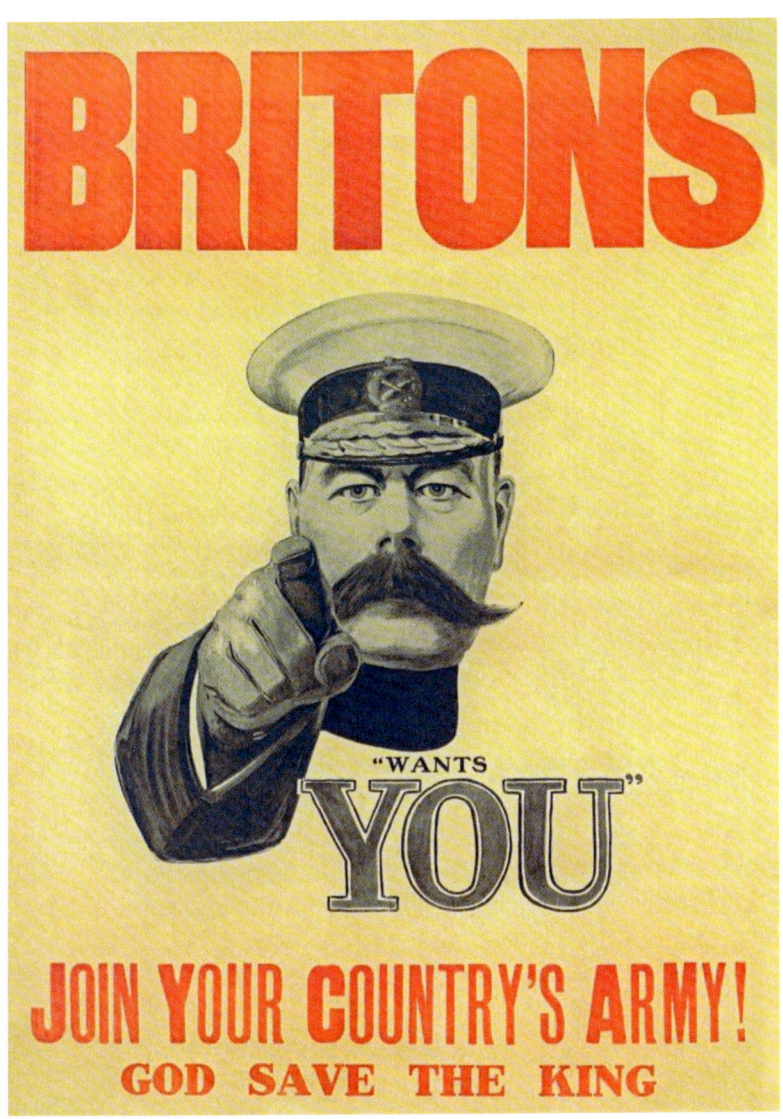

Lord Kitchener Wants You

This iconic image of the Great War played such a large part in recruitment for Kitchener's Army.

Introduction

The Countryman at War was my father, who worked on the land for all of his life, apart from the years that he spent on military service. In 1915, he volunteered to join the army, did his duty for King and Country and then returned to the job he had left. Although he had endured all the horrors of the Great War, he did not talk much about it. One assumes that it was just too difficult to communicate his combat experience to those who had not known it.

The account that follows is based on a number of sources but many of them are taken from the personal recollections of my father. He wrote a brief account of his wartime experiences in a diary written some years after the end of hostilities and direct quotations from these memoirs are shown in green italics.

Pte 1228 W. S. Batey

Other sources include a comprehensive account of the 18th Battalion written by Lieutenant-Colonel John Shakespear and published in 1920. A bibliography appears on page 47 with other sources consulted.

My father, William Smith Batey, was born in 1893 at Codley Gate, near Bardon Mill, a farm on the Roman Stanegate and in the shadow of the Roman fort of Vindolanda. At that time there were no cars, buses or lorries on the roads – only horse transport and the network of railways. Most of his childhood, however, was spent in and around Stamfordham, the village where he went to school. Numeracy and literacy skills were well taught up to the age of 14 when he left to work on local farms.

By the start of the 20th century, however, public transport had begun to develop and, as a young man, my father would have made occasional social trips to Newcastle. On one of these trips, on Saturday 9th January 1915, when he was 21, he signed up to join the army.

Pte 1228 W. S. Batey

There may have been a recruiting parade going through the town perhaps with a band playing. Or maybe the posters showing the appeal by Lord Kitchener 'Your Country Needs You' might have been enough.

The Newcastle and Gateshead Incorporated Chamber of Commerce made one of the most significant contributions nationally by any private body in forming three battalions of the Kitchener's New Armies. Following the raising of the

16th and 17th Battalions, the Chamber found that it had a surplus of volunteers willing to serve. Permission was granted to form a further battalion – the 18th Battalion Northumberland Fusiliers, which was formed on 14th October 1914. Like the earlier Battalions, the 18th were funded, accommodated, equipped and fed until early in 1915 by the Chamber when the War Office took over responsibility. The Chamber was subsequently reimbursed for almost all their financial outlay but the formation and management of more than 5,000 men overall – in the three battalions – was a major contribution to the successful raising of Kitchener's New Armies. No one doubted the enthusiasm of the volunteers but some might have to wait weeks or even months for their uniforms and weapons.

The decision of my father to sign up was unusual, as no other farm men from his area had volunteered. When he returned home, the reaction of his family, friends, colleagues and employer is not known. Indeed, agriculture at that time was much in favour with an urgent demand to feed the nation. It is unlikely that he had a choice and was enrolled into the 18th Battalion Northumberland Fusiliers, one of the many Battalions formed on Tyneside, and became Private 1228 W. S. Batey. When he joined on 9th January 1915, he probably assumed that this would be an Infantry Battalion but, on 8th February, it was designated to be a Pioneer Battalion. His chances of survival improved considerably, although he would be unaware of this at the time. He was inoculated on 16th and 27th February against typhoid and vaccinated against smallpox on 26th March.

It would have been a dramatic change of lifestyle for my father to move from working with life-long friends on a farm to the discipline of army life. There were no other farm lads in the Battalion. Most would be miners, shipyard workers or other tradesmen from Tyneside. A soldier would keep spare clothes and all his personal belongings, including a Bible, in a kitbag. It was thought vital that each man should have a Bible and every one of the 5.7 million British soldiers, sailors and airmen who joined up were issued with a copy of the New Testament, which was prefaced with a message from Field Marshall Lord Roberts dated 25th August 1914.

LORD ROBERTS'S MESSAGE.

"I ask you to put your trust in God. He will watch over you and strengthen you. You will find in this little Book guidance when you are in health, comfort when you are in sickness, and strength when you are in adversity".

It is not surprising that the words inside the front cover are perhaps difficult to read because Lord Roberts wrote the message by hand. He was 81 at the time and died later that year on 14th November, aged 82.

Orders required that buttons and badges were to be polished, a uniform to be laundered and looked after, and a rifle to be disassembled, cleaned, reassembled and generally maintained ready for daily inspection. Everyone in the 18th N.F. Battalion had to grow a moustache. No one knew why but that was the Colonel's stipulation. However, while training in the North East, taking time off was quite casual. One would simply ask the sergeant if it was OK to take the weekend off. Father took full advantage of this arrangement and spent many weekends going by train and bike to stay with his farming friends. Indeed, on one occasion, when he returned to his unit, he found that it had moved at short notice and he had to make his own way from Newcastle to Ripon.

The Pioneer (Service) Battalions

Once the initial advance by German forces into France through Belgium and Luxembourg had been halted, the two sides paused. In autumn 1914, the war of stalemate began and what became known as trench warfare developed. To deal with this new situation, the solution of the War Office was to create a Pioneer Battalion in each Division. These new units were to be trained as conventional infantrymen but with the extra responsibility of digging and maintaining trenches and other engineering works. They were ordered to ensure that at least 50% of their strength should be composed of men used to working with a pick and shovel.[3]

Although formed on 14th October 1914, the 18th Battalion Northumberland Fusiliers did not become a Pioneer Battalion until 8th February 1915. The men grumbled on hearing this news but cheered up when they found out that this entitled them to an extra two pence per day. It would be well earned! *'The work of a Pioneer Battalion was arduous beyond words, dangerous and frequently in offensive operations was purely combatant'.* (Sir Lothian Nicholson, C-in-C 34th Division). *'The Pioneer is a peculiar person, who can be an infantryman one day, a trench digger in "No Man's Land" at night, an expert in barbed wire, a bridge builder, a layer of railway tracks, a sapper, and suchlike. In fact, he is an infantryman and an engineer combined'.* Shakespear, page 9.[1]

The 18th was the Pioneer Battalion within the 34th Division and, in common with the other 12 Battalions, had about 1,000 men: HQ Staff, Transport, Signallers and Machine-Gunners plus four Companies, A, B, C and D, each divided into four Platoons of between 50 and 60 men. My father was in No.10 Platoon within C Company.

Digging practice trenches on Blaeberry Hill above Rothbury

From their formation on 14th October 1914, the 18th spent the next 15 months training for their various tasks. This was done initially around Rothbury and Thropton, where they were made very welcome and the Rev. Frank Hastings staged picture-shows. Lord Armstrong gave them free access to the moorland above the town. Each Company was given a practice length of Front to prepare for defence and the men worked enthusiastically with pick and shovel.

On 21st April 1915, the Battalion was moved by special train to Cramlington; there was a rumour that invasion was a possibility. At this time they had about 400 ancient rifles for their thousand men. Battalion drill was increased in preparation for a review of the whole brigade by King George V on Newcastle Town Moor on 20th May. Both his Majesty and Lord Kitchener complimented the brigadier on the marching and steadiness of the men.

On 3rd June 1915, the Battalion held a recruiting march through Newcastle and saw a special performance at the Hippodrome. See Press Report, pages 45-46, for details.

On 21st July 1915, the Battalion moved for a short stay at Kirkby Malzeard near Ripon and finally to Sutton Veny near Salisbury Plain when they all received their rifles. Their training as Pioneers continued and, during their stay at Salisbury Plain, father won a silver medal for the 34th Division 'Southern Cross Country Running Association' being one of the team of C Company out of 39 teams taking part. He said that practising marching to receive the medal was almost harder than the race itself. Father was a crack shot and took part in competitions. In one, his officer placed a bet against a soldier from another unit. Father scored four bulls and looked up to make a comment about the lower score of the other man. When he shot the last one, he put a bull on to the other target! So the bet was lost.

On 16th October 1915, a ceremony was held at their base at Sutton Veny to mark the first anniversary of the raising of the Battalion. The troops held a parade in the morning under the command of Lieutenant-Colonel John Shakespear and the rest of the day was occupied with a programme of sports, including wire entanglements, sandbag and bomb-throwing competitions and cross-country runs. Speeches were made by a large party of Newcastle officials, including George Renwick, vice-chairman of the Newcastle & Gateshead Chamber of Commerce Military Committee. The day ended with a smoking concert in the Y.M.C.A. Hut.

A soldier wore a khaki jacket of wool serge with two large breast pockets and two on the side, trousers held up with braces and tucked into puttees wrapped round the lower leg from the top of leather boots to the knee. A peaked hat displayed the Regimental badge. When on the march, held on with webbing, were 25 kg of attachments: a water bottle, a small haversack, ammunition, a steel helmet, a bayonet in a pouch, a trenching tool, a mess tin, a cape and a gas mask. Personal hygiene was important. The daily shave, with a cut-throat razor, required a steady hand. In all the photographs showing infantry in battle, no soldier was ever seen with a three-day stubble.

A soldier, who had been assessed 'officially' as wounded, was permitted to wear a vertical stripe on the left cuff. These were introduced on 6th July 1916, Army Order 249, for those soldiers who had been wounded, gassed or shell shocked, as a consequence of enemy action, and was intentionally associated with heroism and sacrifice. My father was allowed to wear the stripe because he had been wounded and gassed at The Somme on 11th September 1916.

In addition, and perhaps most important, every soldier wore around his neck a dog-tag on which his name, number, battalion and religion were imprinted:

W. S. BATEY 1228 18th N. F. PRES (Presbyterian)

France: 1st Tour of Duty

The Battalion embarked from Southampton for France on 7th January 1916. They arrived in Le Havre at 0700, stayed in a rest camp until 1800 and then were entrained, with 35 men in each horsebox, for 24 hours. This was followed by

13

a night march for 7 hours to arrive at 3 a.m. in a straw barn: *"Staples, the most welcome place on earth, tired out."*

They were soon hard at work in and around the trenches: cutting hurdles, draining, loading barges, digging in mortars and field artillery or excavating dugouts. Preparations for The Somme offensive were well under way. Much of their work was done late in the day or at night, often under fire.

To move men and supplies, including ammunition, from the ports to the Front, the existing system of rail tracks was supplemented by hundreds of kilometres of both standard and small gauge railways. Many of the latter would be built and maintained by the Pioneers. Horses and mules were then used to move men, food, fuel and ammunition from the railhead to the Front.

The Trenches

From the end of 1914 until 1918, the line of trenches moved barely more than 8 kilometres in either direction and stretched for 760 kilometres from the Belgian coast to the Swiss border. The British Sector was mostly in a 50 kilometre front in Flanders and Northern France.

The construction of trenches evolved and varied according to the underlying geology. They were usually about 2.5 metres deep and 2 metres wide with the sides secured with wooden supports. To enable men to see over the top, a 60-90 centimetre wide ledge, known as a fire-step, was added to the front side. Wooden duck-boards were placed at the bottom of trenches to give a firmer footing. In wet ground, trenches might be shallower and a parapet of sandbags or earth added to raise the front. Soldiers might be standing in waterlogged trenches for long periods, leading to "trench foot" and the possible amputation of toes, foot or even a leg. This might be prevented by a regular supply of dry footwear.

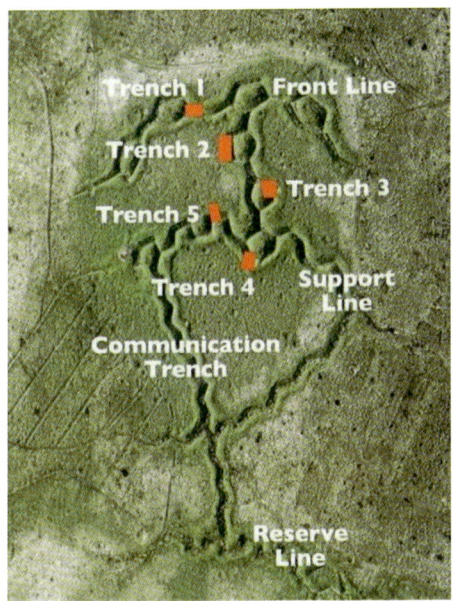

The trenches were not dug in straight lines but zig-zagged with a traverse 'dog leg' every 10 metres or so. There were three lines of trenches, Front, Support and Reserve, with many dugouts cut in the sides to provide shelter from the weather and enemy fire. The Front Line was closest to those of the enemy. Next were the Support Trenches, some 200 metres further back, which were joined to the Front Line by the Communication Trenches. Then 400-500 metres further away were the Reserve Trenches and behind them the Artillery.

Deployment

On an individual level, a typical British infantryman's year could be divided as follows: 15% front line, 10% support line, 30% reserve line, 20% rest, 25% other, such as hospital, travelling, leave, training courses, etc.

Even when in the front line, the typical infantry battalion would only be called upon to engage in fighting a handful of times a year: making an attack, defending against an attack or participating in a raid.

These deployments did not apply to the Pioneer Battalions. They frequently spent long periods at or near the front line and indeed in No man's land in front of the trenches. That was their job – hence the extra two pence per day.

No man's land

'No man's land' between the two opposing front lines might be as narrow as 45 metres or up to 1000 metres, mostly averaging 100-200 metres. This area was usually pitted with shell holes and across it there would be belts of barbed wire up to 1.5 metres high and 30 metres deep. Short trenches or shallow tunnels called saps were dug from the front line out into No man's land. These were used as listening posts and also to have infantrymen closer to the enemy front line to emerge as part of an advance.

In the initial stages of trench warfare, the land lying between the front lines of the opposing forces would simply be open farmland, which was fenced off into fields with patches of trees. There would be scattered farmhouses and small villages. Wheat and maize would have been grown and pastures grazed by dairy cows and sheep. The local farming population was quickly displaced and had to move – taking their household goods, farming implements and livestock with them and no doubt expecting to get back in a few months. As people said, "It will be all over by Christmas."

The typical farmland features would soon begin to disappear as the Artillery began to pound the area. Trees would be reduced to shattered stumps. Soon, devoid of vegetation, bare soil would be exposed on the surface. Any rain would soon saturate the ground and shell holes fill with water that became a significant hazard to foot soldiers.

As the line of trenches became established, No man's land would take on a different perspective, becoming an alien and dangerous zone. The grazing fields became the killing fields. The configuration of the terrain would also become a critical feature, providing either shelter or none to those looking from the 'other side'. Another critical characteristic was the distance between the front lines of the opposing forces. This could be as little as 50 metres or more typically between 100 and 200 metres, sometimes much more.

For many months, No man's land would be deserted. Occasional forays might be made to attempt to capture a soldier of the other side. The arrival or presence of a particular regiment could be useful in predicting whether or not a full scale attack was imminent.

The Pioneer Battalions would soon be familiar with No man's land: going out ahead of the front line and moving across the disputed territory to lay out barbed wire entanglements. Not an easy task in daylight, even more difficult in darkness. They might also be tasked to cut wire laid by the enemy.

However, unless done surreptitiously, this might suggest that an attack was planned. It would not be possible to walk upright into No man's land without attracting the attention of enemy snipers. So creeping quietly close to the ground and using lower parts of the terrain would be the mode of movement.

The Artillery was also aiming to damage or disrupt the trenches of the other side. And, of course, if our trenches were hit, it would be the job of the Pioneers to rebuild them. After the tragic progression of the infantry going 'over the top' and into machine gun fire, those wounded or killed would remain where they fell until rescued by stretcher-bearers. This task was sometimes done by the Pioneers as, for example, in July 1916 after the Infantry Battalions were decimated in their attack on July 1st.

Trench Warfare

Obviously, the most dangerous position in trench warfare was that closest to the enemy – the front line. However, there were long periods, particularly in winter, when there was not a lot of activity. There appeared to be a tacit agreement that, if we didn't trouble them, they would not trouble us. Nevertheless, where the opposing front lines were not far apart, short-range mortars might be used with great effect to inflict damage upon both trench and personnel.

The infantrymen would normally spend a short spell of duty in the front line, perhaps a week or so, before dropping back to the support trenches or away to the rear for a rest. The Pioneers, however, because of the nature of their work, spent longer periods on or near the front line. Many described these 'rest' periods as a misnomer. They were often given extra training and regular drilling. Furthermore, they might have to march, with full pack, for long distances before reaching their base camp, well away from the range of enemy artillery.

A British trench reconstructed

For part of the time during 'rest' periods, father's Platoon was billeted on a farm. He began to help out and undertake work with the French family.

He was treated by them as one of their own and he enjoyed their home cooking. Some of his officers objected to the favours he received but they were given short shrift by the French family and father continued to provide help on the farm.

He may well have been given one or two of the silk postcards that were woven by hand locally and sold to the troops to send back home to Blighty.

During strenuous or dangerous assignments, the sergeant might offer everyone a tot of rum. My father would always decline as he was teetotal – except, that is, on one occasion. He had the 'flu (not the Spanish variety) and was feeling wretched. His mates pooled their tots and insisted that he

19

drank the lot. He did and soon fell into a deep sleep. When he awoke next day, he was bright and cheerful – and all symptoms of the 'flu had gone.

Lice were an ever-present affliction, especially as effective insecticides had not been developed. During rest periods well away from the Front, there were good laundry facilities as well as baths and delousing units. Rats were everywhere too – with more than adequate supplies of food.

Injuries

The main killer in the trenches was artillery fire and accounted for around 75% of known casualties. Even if a soldier was not hit directly by the Artillery, shell fragments and debris had a high chance of wounding those in close proximity to the blast. The second largest contributor to death was gunfire – bullets from rifles and machine-guns.

While the main cause of death in the trenches came from shelling and gunfire, diseases and infections were always present and became a massive burden for all sides as the war progressed. Medical procedures, while considerably more effective than at any previous time in history, were still not very helpful; and antibiotics had not yet been discovered or developed. As a result, infections caught in the trenches often went untreated and could fester until the soldier died.

Medical Support

The medical teams had to prevent disease as well as provide care for the wounded. During the Boer War, only some fifteen years before, mortality from infectious disease (64%), especially typhoid fever, significantly exceeded deaths sustained during fighting (34%).[7] However, by 1914 all troops were inoculated and vaccinated (including father) so that on The Western Front, only 4.5% of deaths were attributable to disease. Most wounded would be given an anti-tetanus injection as routine soon after arriving at an aid post.

Stretcher-bearers struggle through the mud with their casualty

Each battalion had a regimental medical officer (RMO). He had 16 stretcher-bearers attached, increased to 32 during an offensive, whose job it was to go out into No man's land to retrieve the wounded and bring them back to the regimental aid post, close to the front line. Partly because of their proximity to the front line and partly because of a tendency to go out with the stretcher-bearers, the RMO's suffered a high mortality rate.

After assessment by the RMO, a wounded soldier would be transferred to a Casualty Clearing Station for further treatment. These were situated far enough behind the lines to be relatively safe from shelling. From there, they might be moved, if necessary, to a Field Hospital well beyond the range of enemy artillery.

Hypothermia could cause much stress to the wounded, particularly if they had been lying on cold and wet ground for some time. Hot air baths were developed using the heat from a primus stove to flow under a blanket, which was folded over the casualty.

Barbed Wire

Invented in France in 1860, barbed wire was further developed in the United States, where it was used to restrict cattle and secure territory. Used in war for the first time in South Africa, it became an essential and visible feature of trench warfare in the First World War.

The purpose was to entangle the limbs of infantry, forcing them to stop advancing across the battlefield.

Barbed wire was laid in belts 15-30 metres wide often in multiple staked lines or coils only partially stretched out, called concertina wire.

Placing and repairing barbed wire relied on stealth, usually done at night by the Pioneers, who were also tasked with sabotaging enemy wires. The screw picket, invented by the Germans and later adopted by the Allies, was quieter than driving stakes. Barbed wire often stretched in multiple rows for the entire length of a battlefield trench line.

Methods to defeat it were rudimentary. Tanks could flatten it but the wire often became entangled in the tracks. Prolonged artillery bombardment could damage barbed wire but not reliably. The first soldier meeting the wire could jump on to the top of it, hopefully depressing it enough for those that followed to get over him. Wire cutters, designed for the thinner native product, were unable to cope with the heavier gauge German wire.

More than a million miles of barbed wire were laid on the Western Front between 1914 and 1918. After the war, 448 million yards of barbed wire had to be removed from the trench area.

The Battle of The Somme

The 'Somme' was by far the largest battle of WWI so far. Initially, it was to begin towards the end of June 1916 but was delayed until 1st July. It was conducted mostly along a 50 kilometre front between Amiens and Peronne. A total of 129 Infantry Battalions took part with about 100,000 men, two thirds of whom went 'over the top' at 0730 on 1st July, with the rest following later that morning.

"Fix bayonets"

By the evening of the first day of battle, the British Army had suffered unprecedented losses: 60,000 casualties of whom 20,000 had died, more than the combined losses of The Crimean, Boer and Korean Wars. It was eight times more expensive in human life than Waterloo. When the weather stopped the Battle of The Somme in November, the Allies had advanced just ten kilometres.

Within weeks of their arrival in January 1916, members of the 18th N.F. were heavily involved in preparations for The Somme. Beginning with father's own words:

"Under heavy shell fire Feb. 12th at Armentières. Time spent in repairing trenches and laying railway. Left April 8th. 4 days march for a rest. Squad drill for 4 days then entrained at St. Omer for Albert. April 19th: After its move to Albert, the battalion worked on laying a tramway, preparing deep dugouts, and deep emplacements for medium trench mortars."

When working in the forward trenches, often in open country, the Gunners pestered the Pioneers to make observation posts by burrowing a tunnel out from a communication trench ending in a chamber and so providing a loophole to command a view of the enemy front line.

In June 1916, the men of C Company (my father's) were then allocated one of their most dangerous and arduous tasks – to hold the front line. Again, in father's own words:

"Went to hold the trenches. June 23rd: heavy bombardment."

To say 'heavy bombardment' was an understatement. The noise was terrific and could be heard across the Channel in England.[5] The barrage was incessant and the largest of the war so far. It began at 0400 on 24th June and lasted until 0730 on 1st July, with 1.5 million shells being fired.

Many were duds and two thirds were shrapnel rather than high explosives.[4] So, on 1st July, most of the German trenches and their deep dugouts along the front line opposite the British Sector were intact.

It is recorded that the four Platoons of C Company (including my father's) were employed to hold the front line at 'The Glory Hole' opposite the village of La Boisselle continuously for 10 days from 23rd June, not leaving until the evening of 1st July. The opposing lines here were closer together than anywhere else on the Western Front, no more than 45 metres apart.[1]

The men would have to eat and sleep in the trenches and dugouts. During this spell of duty, a shell hit their trench and two men were killed. During this 10-day tour of duty in "The Glory Hole', C Company earned five Military Medals.

The depth and quality of the German trenches (as illustrated above) came as a big surprise to the British forces when they eventually took possession of them.

25

Not far across the German lines, they would have had a direct view, two minutes before zero hour, of two huge mines exploding under the German lines, the Y Sap and the second called Lochnagar. The latter created a great burst of flame and debris and the shock waves were such that some soldiers at a distance of 250 metres suffered leg fractures.[2] An aerial patrol recorded that 'The earthy column rose higher and higher to reach almost four thousand feet'.[6] These would no doubt have given much encouragement to the men of the 34th Division. The massive Lochnagar crater still remains here today, now privately owned after being purchased by Mr. Richard Dunning MBE to prevent it from being filled in and to preserve it for all time.

The men would have been in their dugouts as the Infantry Battalions of the 34th Division lined up and they would watch them go 'over the top' walking over open country towards the enemy lines, many to be mown down. The objective of the Infantry Battalions' advance was to capture the village of La Boisselle, which they achieved after three days of bitter fighting but sustained heavy losses. The thirteen battalions all suffered very heavily on that first day.[2] The 23rd N.F. Battalion (4th Tyneside Scottish) had 629 casualties and the 24th N.F. (1st Tyneside Irish) had 620. The total casualties of the 34th Division were the highest of all the divisions engaged on that fateful day, losing a staggering 6,380 officers and men. The CO of the 18th however, reported that *'Considering how we had been wandering about the battle-field for five days under fire more or less all the time, our losses were ridiculously small. We had 14 killed and 87 wounded, of whom 10 were still at duty'.* Shakespear, page 47.[1] They embussed about 8 p.m. on 6th July to drive away through Albert to the rear for a well-earned 'rest'.

It is not surprising to find that, as you approach the present day village of La Boisselle, you will see a large stone seat, named The Tyneside Memorial.

All the summer of 1916, the 18th Battalion continued its work on The Somme. Father records in his diary, rather laconically on 11th September:

"Wounded and gassed in No Man's Land covering party to the Gordons."

A piece of shrapnel had penetrated his shoulder and he was unable to put on his gas mask so got a full lungful of chlorine gas until his comrades were able to put on his mask. He was rendered unconscious and stretchered out to the Northumbrian's Field Hospital. He remembers coming round and being given oxygen through a mask. A nurse was moving along a line of similar casualties. He would then gradually pass out until the next whiff of oxygen. After three days there, father records:

"2 days in Casualty Clearing Station." He then went to the Canadian General Hospital Etaples. *"Left on Sept. 20th for Blighty. Arrived Queen Mary's Military Hospital, Whalley, near Blackburn on 21st Sept. 1916. Very comfortable and well looked after. Went to Queen's Park Hill Hospital, Blackburn, on Oct. 2nd. Left Blackburn Oct. 20th for 9 days leave."*

France: 2nd Tour of Duty

My father reported for duty in Newcastle on October 30th 1916 and, after a period of light duties, sailed for France on March 8th to rejoin his Battalion on April 14th 1917.

On one occasion, my father was posted as 'missing believed killed'. In the confusion in No man's land, however, he simply had become lost and disorientated, taking a few days to find his way back to his unit.

On June 6th 1917, during one attack, he was completely buried in a trench when a shell exploded nearby. One of his mates, Ernie Richardson, realised what had happened, pointed to the spot and began digging after calling out "Come on laads, Willy's under there."

After scrabbling around, they found his head, cleared his mouth and dug him out, unconscious. After several weeks in hospitals in France and three weeks of light duties, he had a Medical Board on 23rd July and was certified fit and returned for duty with his unit on 26th. For a while, he was escorting prisoners of war, away from the Front.

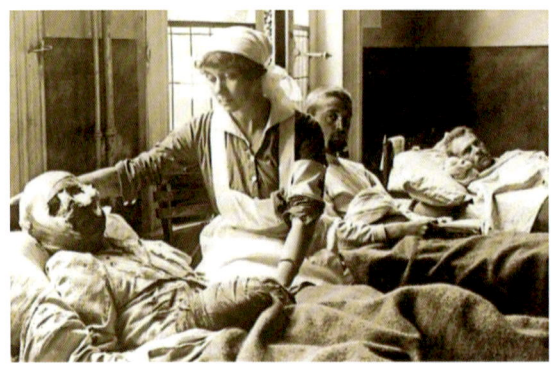
After all that his body had gone through during the previous months, it is not surprising that he became very ill when hit by dysentery a few weeks later.

After a spell in hospital in France, my father was repatriated. He records:

"Went into No. 24 General Hospital 1st August 1917, Dysentery. Arrived in Blighty August 17th, Stepping Hill, near Stockport, then to Barton-on-Sea, Sept 16th. Very quiet place."

To help his recuperation, he had several spells of extended home leave, going back to visit farming friends in the Stamfordham area. He was at home for Christmas 1917 and spent the three-day New Year break at Brixter Hill Farm where he also spent two special leaves in March 1918.

After being judged medically fit for active service, he had a week's leave in early April 1918 and on 9th went to Grantham to transfer to the Machine Gun Corps (MGC) and became Driver 144896. It appears that he was not considered strong enough to rejoin the Pioneers. On 11th April, he was sent to Belton Park camp for transport training and, on 1st July, joined the 16th (Service) Battalion N.F. and was posted to D Company. He was able to see his brother Marley on special leave between 22th and 25th June.

The Battalion left Grantham on 10th July for Southampton and arrived in Le Havre, France, at 5 p.m. on 16th July 1918. This was a quieter period after the German advance on Paris in March 1918 had been repulsed. Over the next five weeks, the troops passed through several French towns and arrived on 22nd August at Barlin, which father describes as a fine town. *"Went up line occasionally, very quiet part."* His Battalion moved to Vaudricourt on September 22nd *"another fine place. Had a good time. Went up line to La Buissière October 3rd."* My father gives no details about his duties as a Driver but his experience with horses would have been vital.

29

Farmers had been expected to 'volunteer' horses for war service but most were conscripted, as in the film "War Horse". In the initial stages of the War, the plan was for Cavalry Regiments to follow on after the Infantry had broken through enemy lines. After trench warfare developed into a stalemate, horses were never fully deployed. They and their riders had no chance against the machine guns, barbed wire and shrapnel.

Horses and mules, however, remained an integral part of the transport system, moving troops, munitions, food and other supplies from the railhead to the Front. It is estimated that one million horses were sent to France but only 62,000 returned. At the end of the War, most were sold off in France and horsepower became horsemeat.

Horses, carts and men could sink into the brown morass of mud

In my father's box of mementos, there is a pair of spurs, which are not part of the kit for a Pioneer and seem to confirm his role as a Driver in the MGC. It is a bit ironic that, despite his farm experience of working with horses, this skill was used only in the last few months of his war service while with the MGC.

Fatalities

The records show that, of the 231 men of C Company who disembarked at Le Havre in January 1916, 39 were killed (one in six) and a further 70 were wounded, giving total casualties of almost 50%. Most were killed on The Somme: 14 on 1st and 2nd July and 19 between 28th August and 9th September.

During The Somme Campaign, the highest recorded casualties (killed and wounded) were those incurred by the 34th Division: 6,380. The Pioneer Battalions lost, on average, 42 killed and the Infantry Battalions 190.

Demobilisation

My father was discharged from war service and transferred to the Reserve on 25th February 1919.

Upon demobilisation, soldiers were usually transferred to the Reserve because the document signed on 11th November 1918 was a truce. The peace treaty would be signed at Versailles on 28th June 1919. The demobilisation certificate proved that a man had "done his bit" for King and Country and was a strong recommendation, even a prerequisite, for getting employment back home in Blighty.

My father's Certificate of Transfer to Reserve 25.02.1919

Post-War Life

After demobilisation on 25th February 1919, my father returned to farm work at The Heugh near Stamfordham. In the 1920s, the Gledson family gave up the farm. Miss Gledson moved to a smaller unit at The Medburn with my father as worker / manager.

When he planned to marry the school teacher at nearby Dalton School, Miss Gledson helped him to take on the tenancy of Broomhill Farm, in May 1932, an upland farm bordering the A68 just south of West Woodburn.

Although their wedding was fourteen years after the end of the War, Captain Herbert J. Armstrong, one of the Company Commanders, sent him a warm letter of congratulation and a present of a silver cruet, which is still with the family.

In 1939, he moved to better quality land at Gilchesters Farm near Stamfordham and retired from there in 1959 to live in Wylam.

Some 20 years after the end of the War, when in his 50s, I recall that, on foggy nights, father would be in great distress, sitting up in bed, with his chest heaving, and gasping for breath. He took a medicine called Angier's Emulsion but it had little effect. This we know now would be a classic case of a Pavlovian reaction to the gas attack in 1916.

The symptoms gradually declined and eventually he could endure a foggy night with no reaction.

During investigations, when in his 50s, for a suspected ulcer, X-rays located shrapnel lodged near his stomach; the pieces had migrated from the shoulder. No action was taken as the metal did not appear to be doing any harm.

Ernie Richardson, the friend who had saved his life when he was buried in a trench on 6th June 1917, came to see him regularly at Wylam in the 1960s after they had both retired.

In the 1950s and 1960s, he went regularly to the annual reunion of 18th Battalion Comrades League in Newcastle, until there were too few members left. This would have provided an opportunity to share experiences, which otherwise might not have been available to them. An account of the reunions was published in "The Chequers" annually and a copy for 1959/60 remains in the family.

My father died in Hexham Memorial Hospital in 1979 at the age of 85.

Some of my father's mementos of his service in the Great War.

SUMMARY OF MY FATHER'S WAR SERVICE

Joined 11/01/1915 with training for 1 year

Arrived France 08/01/1916

The Somme, wounded and gassed 11/09/1916

Hospital and recuperation 7 months

Rejoined Battalion 14/04/1917

Buried 06/06/1917

Light duties until 26/07/1917

Dysentery 01/08/1917

Repatriated 17/08/1917

Transferred MGC 09/04/1918

Returned to France 16/07/1918

Discharged 25/02/1919 after 4 years and 2 weeks of war service

Although wounded and gassed, my father was one of the fortunate ones who was able to return to his former life.

A Roll of Honour follows on pages 39 and 40 and gives the names of the fatalities in the 18th Battalion Northumberland Fusiliers at the Battle of The Somme.

IN FLANDERS FIELDS

3rd May 1915

In Flanders fields, the poppies blow
Between the crosses, row on row,
That mark our place; and in the sky
The larks, still bravely singing, fly
Scarce heard amid the guns below.

We are the Dead. Short days ago
We lived, felt dawn, saw sunset glow,
Loved and were loved, and now we lie
In Flanders fields.

Take up our quarrel with the foe:
To you from failing hands we throw
The torch; be yours to hold it high.
If ye break faith with us who die,
We shall not sleep, though poppies grow
In Flanders Fields.

Lieut.-Colonel John McCrae, M. D. 1872-1918

Epilogue

In 2013, to celebrate my 80th year, my son Dan took me to The Western Front to explore the area where my father had fought in WW1. We stayed in Albert. It is difficult to find words that adequately describe our reactions. Sobering, shocking, admiration, futility and overall What a Waste come to mind.

Our first sighting was The Tyneside Memorial seat on the edge of the road leading into La Boisselle: we also saw memorials to the 34th and 19th Divisions near the Church. It was quite evocative to reflect that my father had fought here and would have looked at the gently rolling countryside from a very different perspective.

The Lochnagar Crater

Driving up through the village, there is a sign to the car park for the Lochnagar Crater. Even though it is over 100 years since it was formed, it remains an impressive sight, although fully grassed over. When the 27 tons of ammonal exploded at 0728 on 1st July 2016, the mine made a crater 100 metres across and 21 metres deep, including a lip 4.6 metres high. This is the largest crater made by man in anger in history. The massive explosion would have been heard, seen and felt by my father whose Company was manning the front line less than two kilometres away.

We moved on to the Thiepval Memorial. It was deeply moving to stand within the enormous arch and examine the names of over 72,000 soldiers who had died and had no known grave. There were sixteen from the 18th Battalion.

The Thiepval Memorial

Although expecting to see war graves, the sheer number was sobering, all cared for so beautifully by the War Graves Commission. At one of the largest cemeteries, we joined the staff and pupils from a school in Lancashire for a picnic lunch. They told us that a party from their school came every year. It was good to hear.

THE BATTLE OF THE SOMME
ROLL OF HONOUR
18th Battalion Northumberland Fusiliers

Pte James AGNEW, Died of wounds 11.07.1916, Age 35

LCpl John Walter ASHTON, Killed in action 07.09.1916, Age 32

Cpl Oswald Charles ASH, Killed in action 31.08.1916, Age 21

Pte Frederick BATIE, Killed in action 05.09.1916, Age 20 *

LCpl George Ernest BRIGGS, Killed in action 08.09.1916, Age 29

Pte John Reavely BROWN, Died of wounds 02.07.1916, Age 32

Pte John COLLINGWOOD, Killed in action 01.07.1916, Age 23 *

Lt Henry Whitaker COOMBS, Died of wounds 02.07.1916, Age 23

Pte John DENT, Killed in action 01.07.1916, Age 21

Pte Joseph DICK, Killed in action 04.09.1916, Age 29 *

Pte John Thomas DOUGLAS, Killed in action 10.09.1916, Age 21

Pte Charles Henry DUGGAN, Killed in action 01.07.1916, Age 25 *

Sgt Allan EDGAR, Killed in action 01.09.1916, Age 24

Pte Thomas FAIRBAIRN, Died of wounds 03.09.1916, Age 26

Pte John GARRITY, Killed in action 01.07.1916, Age 23 *

Pte Thomas GUSTARD, Killed in action 01.07.1916, Age 30 *

LCpl John HALL, Died of wounds 29.06.1916, Age 25

Pte George HAMMELL, Killed in action 31.08.1916, Age 24

Pte George HART, Killed in action 01.07.1916, Age 16 *

Pte Ernest James JUDE, Died of wounds 29.06.1916, Age 18

Pte Anthony KNOX, Killed in action 26.09.1916, Age 21 *

Pte John George KYLE, Killed in action 07.10.1916, Age 27

Pte Joseph LAMBERTON, Killed in action 01.07.1916, Age 20 *

Pte Alexander MOLE, Died of wounds 11.09.1916, Age 34
Pte Thomas MONKHOUSE, Killed in action 01.07.1916, Age 27 *
Pte John OXLEY, Killed in action 01.07.1916, Age 38
LCpl William POTTS, Died of wounds 08.09.1916, Age 25
Pte Charles Edward REED, Died of wounds 08.09.1916, Age 24
Pte Charles William RIDDLE, Killed in action 01.07.1916, Age 23 *
Pte John S. T. ROBERTSON, Died of wounds 07.09.1916, Age 28
Pte John W. ROBERTSON, Died of wounds 03.09.1916, Age 29
LCpl Fredk. RUTHERFORD, Killed in action 01.07.1916, Age 29
Pte James SHORT, Died of wounds 08.09.1916, Age 19
Pte Robert SNOWDEN, Killed in action 01.07.1916, Age 34 *
Pte James STEPHENSON, Killed in action 01.07.1916, Age 21 *
Pte John Thomas STOTT, Killed in action 16.09.1916, Age 36
LCpl Thomas William TAYLOR, Killed in action 31.08.1916, Age 31
Pte James B. THOMSON, Killed in action 04.09.1916, Age 24 *
Pte Henry WAKE, Killed in action 09.09.1916, Age 24 *
LCpl Mark Leck WATSON, Killed in action 01.09.1916, Age 21
LCpl John WILDE, Killed in action 09.09.1916, Age 24 *

* = a soldier with no known grave, one of the Missing of The Somme, who is commemorated on the Thiepval Memorial, the largest Commonwealth Memorial to the Missing in the world.

A PROUD DAY FOR THE SERVICE BATTALIONS

*The Prince of Wales unveils the War Memorial
at Newcastle upon Tyne Thursday 5th July 1923*

*It aroused the Prince's comment that
"It was a beautiful thing, all alive"*

Image by courtesy of Illustrated London News/Mary Evans Picture Library

A LASTING MEMORIAL TO THE SERVICE BATTALIONS

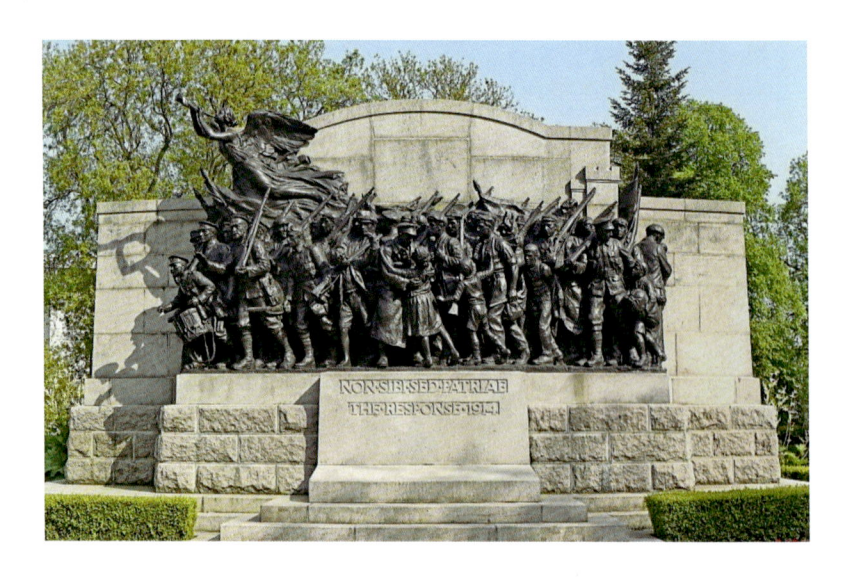

Modern views of the Renwick memorial, Newcastle upon Tyne

The Prince of Wales unveils the Renwick War Memorial, 5th July 1923

In the presence of a distinguished company, his Royal Highness unveiled the striking monument, given to the city by Sir George and Lady Renwick, to commemorate the raising of the B Company, 9th Battalion, and the 16th, 18th, and 19th Service Battalions of the Northumberland Fusiliers by the Newcastle and Gateshead Chamber of Commerce.

The monument consists of a large processional bronze group, against a background of granite, depicting types of Tyneside workers answering the call to the colours. The procession is headed by the Northumberland Fusiliers and two drummer boys. Children are represented as running along, cheering their fathers and brothers, and helping to carry rifles and kit; there is a husband and father bidding goodbye to his wife and children; and a young soldier, embracing his sister, forms the central feature of the group.

On the base of the pedestal are the words: "Non sibi sed Patriae" (Not for themselves but for their Country) and, over and above all, is a figure symbolising the fame of the regiment. The back of the monument has been decoratively treated. St. George, supported by sea horses, is the central figure, with a soldier in the uniform of 1674, the year the regiment was enrolled, on the right, and, on the left, another in the uniform of 1919. The figures are sculptured in granite and below is the commemorative inscription.

After the unveiling ceremony, the Prince proceeded to the Commercial Exchange at the Guildhall where he congratulated everyone most sincerely on their wonderful record in the Great War.

The Yorkshire Post, Friday, 6th July, 1923

The Renwick War Memorial

Further details and a special Postage Stamp

The Response 1914 is considered to be one of the finest war memorials in the country. It came as no surprise, therefore, that it appeared on one of the six Royal Mail postage stamps that were launched on Monday 28 July 2014 to commemorate the centenary of the First World War. A special wreath laying ceremony followed on 2nd August to mark the occasion.

The memorial stands in the public gardens to the north of the Church of St. Thomas the Martyr in Barras Bridge, Newcastle upon Tyne, and to the west of Newcastle Civic Centre.

It was commissioned by Sir George and Lady Renwick and given to the city in 1923 to commemorate three events: the raising of the Commercial Battalion of the Northumberland Fusiliers; the return of the five Renwick sons from the War; and Sir George Renwick's attainment of 50 years of commercial life on Newcastle Quayside.

The memorial was designed by Sir William Goscombe John RA (1860-1952) who was a prolific Welsh sculptor and known for his many public memorials.

After restoration, the memorial was rededicated on 25th October 2007 in the presence of Prince Philip, Duke of Edinburgh, and the descendants of the Renwick family. It achieved listed status in 1971 and was awarded Grade I listed status in October 2014.

44

Parade of "The Commercials"

through Newcastle, 3rd June 1915

In connection with the visit to Newcastle today of the 18th (Service) Battalion Northumberland Fusiliers, under the command of Lieutenant-Colonel John Shakespear, D.S.O., C.I.E., the route to be taken will be by Percy Street, Blackett Street, Clayton Street, Central Station, Collingwood Street, Mosley Street, Grey Street, Market Street, Pilgrim Street, and Northumberland Street to the Hippodrome.

The battalion will pass the War Memorial in Barras Bridge at about 12.15 p.m. and their march through the city will bring them to the Hippodrome at about 12.45 p.m. Sergeants of the battalion will be placed at various points along the line of route with a view to obtaining the sixty recruits required to bring this battalion up to its full strength. Intending recruits may also have their names registered in the entrance hall of the theatre while the entertainment is in progress.

After the Lord Major has taken a salute at the Town Hall at 12.30 p.m., he will proceed to the Hippodrome, where lunch will be provided by the Military Committee, after which his Lordship will briefly address the men prior to the commencement of the performance.

Seventy wounded soldiers will be present at the Hippodrome for the entertainment which is to be given through the courtesy of the manager, Mr. Bebby. The wounded soldiers will arrive at the theatre about 1.45 p.m. and will be accommodated in reserved seats in the front of the theatre.

Recruiting is fairly brisk in Newcastle, though the response to the call to arms is as yet nothing like adequate, having regard to the large number of men required to fill local units. Scores are coming forward where hundreds are needed, there being huge gaps to fill in the Territorial infantry battalions; while more men are wanted for the Commercial, Scottish and Irish battalions and for the reserves of the Regular battalions of the Northumberland Fusiliers and the Durham Light Infantry.

For the transport sections of the Army Service Corps men are also required. They should present themselves at the recruiting office, New Bridge Street, Newcastle, with references to show that they are accustomed to horses and can drive a pair, and also those amongst them who are married, with particulars as to the date of their marriage and the birth of their children.

When attested, recruits will be sent to Bradford, where they are further examined and, if passed, are retained as drivers. If recruits fail to pass the second examination, they can still be retained for the Army Service Corps as loaders or any other branch of the regiment suitable, or, on the other hand, they are at perfect liberty to return to their home.

Wheelwrights and smiths are urgently required for the Army Service Corps and Royal Artillery and other mounted units. The rate of pay is five shillings a day, together with full separation allowance. Recruits for these positions must bring references relating to their trade. When attested, they will be dispatched to Woolwich for examination and afterwards appointed to the various mounted units, if satisfactory. Should they fail to pass the second examination, the recruits may return to their homes or join any other regiment.

There is no doubt that the mounted branches of the service find most popularity. It may be pointed out that there are still openings in these. A local unit that is in want of recruits is the 1st Northumbrian Brigade, R.F.A (Second Line) whose headquarters are in Barrack Road, Newcastle.

The Newcastle Daily Journal, Thursday, 3rd June 1915

Bibliography and other Sources consulted

1. Historical Records of the 18th Battalion Northumberland Fusiliers (1920), Lieut.-Colonel John Shakespear, Chamber of Commerce, Newcastle upon Tyne.

2. One Day on The Somme 1st July 1916 (2007), Barry Cuttell, GMS Enterprises.

3. Pioneer Battalions in the Great War (1997), K. W. Mitchinson, Pen and Sword Military books.

4. 1914-1918 The History of the First World War (2004), David Stevenson, Allen Lane.

5. 1914-18 The Great War and the Shaping of the 20th Century (1996), J. Winter and B. Baggett, BBC Books.

6. SOMME: Major & Mrs Holt's battlefield guide, Tonie and Valmai Holt (2003), Pen and Sword Military.

7. War Surgery 1914-18, edited by Thomas Scotland and Steven Hays (2012), Helion & Company Ltd.

8. The Otterburn Ranges, All Quiet on the Western Front (n.d.), Defence Estates.

9. What Tommy took to War 1914-1918 (2014), Peter Doyle & Chris Foster, Shire Publications Ltd.

Life in the trenches has been portrayed in the film The Trench (William Boyd 1999) and in the screen play and film War Horse (Spielberg 2011). A good example of a dugout in the front line is shown in the TV series Blackadder goes Forth.

Most images are taken from the family collection of Thomas Batey or the archives of the Heritage Centre, Bellingham. Others are believed to be in the public domain.

THROUGH A SOLDIER'S EYES

These pictures of the Great War are some of the hundreds that were produced as stereographs by the Realistic Travels Company of London for the enlightenment of the civilian population. Stereographs were two pictures of the same scene taken at slightly different angles and mounted side by side on a card to produce a 3D effect when seen through a viewer rather like a pair of binoculars.

Some were taken at training camps, such as those that Private W. S. Batey experienced as a new recruit, but many were taken in France, especially those showing the destruction wrought by warfare on an industrial scale.

Whatever their origin, these pictures and their captions give an insight into fighting at the Front in the Great War.

Allied tanks break down the belts of barbed wire and carry consternation to the enemy at Cambrai

A staff officer from G H Q in a dugout reviews details before the opening of our offensive

In a firing bay at Passchendaele we repulse repeated enemy counter-attacks of great fury

A cavalry ammunition park in a Flanders Lane

The Seaforths snatch an hour's respite before going over the top

Officers of the Royal Army Medical Corps at their dressing station at Monchy attend to wounded soldiers from the battle zone

Bombing the enemy out of their deep dugouts near Martinpuich during the allied advance on The Somme

Allies break through the Hindenburg Line and seize a blockhouse shattered by our guns at Croisilles

Off on a night raid our troops steal into the inky darkness of No man's land near Messines

Attending to the wounded on the Menin Road, Ypres, during strenuous struggles around Zonnebeke

A trench mortar hurls a shell which is seen by our troops in mid-air on its deadly flight

A postcard of the period expressing joy in the victory that the Northumberland Fusiliers helped to win.

54